When Penguins
CROSS THE ICE

THE EMPEROR PENGUIN MIGRATION

by Sharon Katz Cooper

illustrated by Tom Leonard

raintree
a Capstone company — publishers for children

Raintree is an imprint of Capstone Global Library Limited, a company incorporated in England and Wales having its registered office at 7 Pilgrim Street, London, EC4V 6LB – Registered company number: 6695582

www.raintree.co.uk
myorders@raintree.co.uk

With thanks to our advisers for their expertise, research and advice:

Gerald Kooyman, Research Professor
Scripps Institution of Oceanography, La Jolla, California, USA

Terry Flaherty, PhD, Professor of English
Minnesota State University, Mankato, USA

Editorial Credits
Jill Kalz, editor; Lori Bye, designer; Nathan Gassman, art director; Laura Manthe, production specialist

ISBN 978 1 4747 6467 4
21..20..19..18 17
10 9 8 7 6 5 4 3 2 1

British Library Cataloguing in Publication Data
A full catalogue record for this book is available from the British Library

Photo Credits
The illustrations in this book were created with acrylics.
Image Credit: Shutterstock: Volina, 3 (map)

Printed and bound in India.

EDITOR'S NOTE: Antarctica and the surrounding waters are home to more than 50 colonies of emperor penguins. Every year roughly 200,000 breeding pairs migrate from the sea. Most travel only a few kilometres. But one small group, the Pointe Géologie colony, travels a long way. Its members may walk up to 113 kilometres (70 miles) across the ice. This book tells the story of one of those penguins.

Emperor penguins live in one of the coldest, darkest places on Earth – Antarctica. In winter, temperatures may drop to minus 40 degrees Celsius (minus 40 degrees Fahrenheit). Each year thousands of emperor penguins make an amazing journey across the ice. They leave the edge of the sea and travel to places with no food and very little warmth. Why is this migration so important to them?

ANTARCTICA

● emperor penguin
breeding ground

0	500	1000	1500	2000 kilometres
0	316	632	948	1264 miles

Pointe Géologie

Splash! The emperor penguin dives into the water. It is February, the end of the Antarctic summer. A hard winter lies ahead. To prepare for it, the penguin fills himself up with fish and krill.

March arrives. Days get shorter. It is time for the penguin to leave the sea.

A long line of male and female emperor penguins stretches across the ice. He joins them, marching single file. Sometimes he slides on his belly to save energy.

A few days later, the penguin reaches the breeding ground. Thousands more arrive soon. One of the female penguins catches his eye. The two get to know each other. After about one month, they mate.

In late May the female lays one egg. The egg is the reason the penguins have travelled so far. Carefully the male takes the egg from the female. This is a big moment. If the egg sits too long on the icy ground, the chick inside the shell will die.

The male penguin covers the egg with his brood pouch. Once the egg is safe, his mate heads off back to the open sea. The journey is long, but she must go. There is no way of getting food at the breeding ground. For about two months, the mother penguin will eat all she can. Then she will return to help raise her chick.

The male penguin stays behind. He and the other males stand together with their eggs on their feet. They take turns being on the outside of the group, where it is coldest. Through the darkest and windiest winter days, they huddle to keep the eggs warm. They eat nothing at all.

Peck, peck! Crack! After about 70 days, the egg hatches. Out wiggles a hungry baby penguin!

Even though the father penguin has not eaten for nearly four months, his body does something amazing. It makes crop milk. This special milk is made inside the father penguin's throat and fed to the chick by mouth.

In August the mother penguin returns.
Thousands of other penguins are already there.
To find her mate, she calls out. He calls back.
Straight away the mother penguin takes over
feeding the chick. She gives it partly eaten food
from her stomach.

Now, at last, the father penguin is able to
leave for the sea to fill his own stomach!

The mother and father penguins take turns caring for their chick. Once it is about 50 days old, the chick can be left alone for a time. It huddles together with other chicks in a crèche while its parents search for food.

December comes, and so does summer! A lot of the ice by the edge of the sea melts. It is now not so far to walk from the breeding ground to the sea.

The parent penguins return to the sea. Their young are ready to be on their own. In a few weeks, they too will dive into the water.

Emperor Penguin Fast Facts

Scientific name: *Aptenodytes forsteri*

Height: about 99 centimetres (39 inches) tall

Weight: 22–45 kilograms (49–99 pounds)

Life span: 15–20 years

Home: spends about three-quarters of its life in the water

Egg weight (average): 454 grams (1 pound)

Diet: fish, crustaceans, krill, squid

Predators: leopard seals, petrels, skuas

Breath control: can stay under water for nearly 28 minutes

Migration: from a few kilometres up to 113 kilometres (70 miles) each way

Group name: colony

Comprehension Questions

1. Why is it important for thousands of emperor penguins to journey across the ice every year?

2. Explain the steps the male emperor penguin takes to keep his egg (and later, his newly hatched chick) safe.

3. What is the purpose of a brood pouch?

Glossary

breeding ground place where penguins go to find mates and raise their chicks

brood pouch flap of feather-covered skin that male penguins use to warm and protect their eggs and chicks

chick young bird

colony large group of animals that live together in the same area

crèche group or cluster of chicks

krill small, shrimp-like animal

mate join together to produce young; a mate is also the male or female partner of a pair of animals

migration movement from one area to another on a regular basis, usually to find food or to produce young

predator animal that hunts other animals

Read More

Amazing Animal Journeys (Great Migrations), Laura Marsh (National Geographic Society, 2010)

Amazing Animal Survivors (Animal Superpowers), John Townsend (Raintree, 2013)

Emperor Penguin (A Day in the Life: Polar Animals), Katie Marsico (Raintree, 2012)

Websites

www.bbc.co.uk/nature/life/Emperor_Penguin
Learn more about emperor penguins, read some fascinating penguin stories and watch some amazing videos on the BBC website.

www.kids.nationalgeographic.com/animals/emperor-penguin
Find lots of information about emperor penguins and their habitat on the National Geographic Kids website.

www.rspb.org.uk
Search under migration on the RSPB website to read about some amazing bird migration journeys.

Index

LOOK OUT FOR ALL THE BOOKS IN THE SERIES:

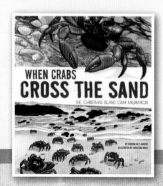
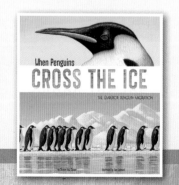
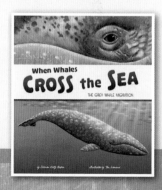